Beyond Self
The Imitation of Christ

Beyond Self
The Imitation of Christ

By Thomas à Kempis

Updated and Paraphrased
by Jason Rowinski

ANCIENT FAITH SERIES

Barefoot Ministries®
Kansas City, Missouri

Copyright 2009 by Barefoot Ministries®

ISBN 978-0-8341-5032-4

Editor: Mike L. Wonch
Assistant Editor: Stephanie L. McNelly
Cover Design: Arthur Cherry
Inside Design: Sharon Page

All Scripture quotations not otherwise designated are from the *Holy Bible, New International Version*® (NIV®). Copyright ©1973, 1978, 1984 by International Bible Society. Used by permission of Zondervan Publishing House. All rights reserved.

From *The Message* (TM). Copyright © 1993. Used by permission of NavPress Publishing Group.

Scripture quotations marked (NLT) are taken from the *Holy Bible, New Living Translation*, copyright © 1996. Used by permission of Tyndale House Publishers, Inc., Wheaton, Illinois 60189. All rights reserved.

Scripture taken from the *Holy Bible, Today's New International Version*™ TNIV®. Copyright © 2001, 2005 by International Bible Society®. All rights reserved worldwide.

From the *New American Standard Bible* (NASB), © 1960, 1962, 1963, 1968, 1971, 1972, 1973, 1975, 1977 by The Lockman Foundation. Used by permission.

Library of Congress Control Number: 2008941221

10 9 8 7 6 5 4 3 2 1

Table of Contents

Dedication	7
Preface	9
A Note About This Book and the Series	13
Book 1: The Basics of the Spiritual Life	**15**
1. *Living Beyond Self means recognizing the emptiness of this world*	17
2. *Living Beyond Self means keeping a humble perspective about yourself*	19
3. *Living Beyond Self means walking the path of truth*	20
4. *Living Beyond Self means thinking about what you do before you do it*	23
5. *Living Beyond Self means meditating on the Bible*	24
6. *Living Beyond Self means balancing your desires*	25
7. *Living Beyond Self means eliminating false hope and pride*	26
8. *Living Beyond Self means choosing close friends wisely*	27
9. *Living Beyond Self means learning to be obedient*	28
10. *Living Beyond Self means being careful with what we say*	29
11. *Living Beyond Self means living peacefully with a passion for spiritual growth*	30
12. *Living Beyond Self means turning adversity into advantage*	32
13. *Living Beyond Self means resisting temptation*	33
14. *Living Beyond Self means not rushing to judgment*	36
15. *Living Beyond Self means that love for others is your main motivation*	37
16. *Living Beyond Self means being patient with other people's imperfections*	38
17. *Living Beyond Self means living the life of a servant*	39
18. *Living Beyond Self means following the footsteps of the Christian saints before us*	40
19. *Living Beyond Self means exercising your faith*	43

20. *Living Beyond Self means learning to love solitude and silence* — 46
21. *Living Beyond Self means developing a spiritually sensitive heart* — 49
22. *Living Beyond Self means understanding the true source of happiness* — 52
23. *Living Beyond Self means having no fear of death* — 55
24. *Living Beyond Self means understanding judgment for sin* — 58
25. *Living Beyond Self means surrendering your whole self to God* — 60

Book 2: Developing a Heart for God — 65

1. *Living Beyond Self means tending to your spiritual heart* — 67
2. *Living Beyond Self means bringing everything to God in humility* — 70
3. *Living Beyond Self means you must be a person of peace* — 71
4. *Living Beyond Self means having a single focus* — 73
5. *Living Beyond Self means trusting in God, not yourself* — 74
6. *Living Beyond Self means experiencing the joy of a good conscience* — 75
7. *Living Beyond Self means loving Jesus more than anyone or anything* — 77
8. *Living Beyond Self means keeping company with Jesus* — 78
9. *Living Beyond Self means finding comfort in God alone* — 80
10. *Living Beyond Self means cultivating gratitude for God's grace* — 83
11. *Living Beyond Self means being counted among the few that truly love the Cross* — 85
12. *Living Beyond Self means following the path of Jesus* — 87

Dedication

This book began as a labor of love shared over E-mails with friends and family—those who have been with me on the journey of Christlikeness. You know who you are and I pray that you will always know how much you mean to me. Each of you has shaped my Christian walk in some way or another and I thank God for you every time I remember you. You are all imitators of Christ and inspire me to imitate Christ too. I look forward to the things to come as we continue on our journey, both in this life and the life to come.

Grace, Peace, and Love,
Jason

Preface

Sometimes we are caught up in thinking that God really can't use us for anything great because we don't have any special gifts. This kind of thinking hinders our spiritual journey in several ways. First, we stop looking for all the amazing ways God wants to work in and through our lives. Second, we underestimate how God intends to use the ordinary stuff of our everyday lives to extend His Kingdom of love in this world. Thankfully, God knows better than we do. In fact, God takes great joy in using people who do not look like much in the eyes of the world but who do great things for Him through their daily faithfulness.

By all accounts, Thomas à Kempis was not an extraordinarily gifted person. He was born Thomas Hammerken in the town of Kempen (which is why he became known as Thomas à Kempis) in 1380 C.E. He entered a monastery at the age of 19 and remained there until his death in 1471 C.E. Thomas's everyday life remained mostly the same over the years. Though the other monks tried to give him leadership positions, he didn't enjoy that kind of ministry; instead, he preferred his quiet time in study and prayer. He devoted his time to prayer, study, copying manuscripts of the Bible, teaching beginning monks, offering Mass, and hearing the confessions of people who came to the monastery. His outer life was not very eventful or exciting; he lived and died a simple monk.

Thomas had a deep and passionate love for Jesus. Out of this love came the devotional book known as *The Imitation of Christ*. (After the Bible, this book is the most widely translated book in Christian literature.) This mediation on the spiritual life has inspired readers from Thomas More and St. Ignatius Loyola to Thomas Merton and Pope John Paul I. To this day, the book is still accepted and loved by people of all religious backgrounds. It is so widely read by so many people because it contains clear instructions for renouncing selfish pursuits and teaches simple Christian spirituality.

One particular theme Thomas repeats throughout *The Imitation of Christ* is the need to trust God's goodness. Many of us feel the need to seek the approval of others, rather than seeking God's presence. Sometimes we make the mistake of needing to feel God's presence in order to think everything is all right. However, Thomas teaches us that we need to trust in God's goodness above everything else, no matter the circumstances in our lives. If people reject us, God still loves us. If we feel like God isn't present with us, we must take Him at His Word and know that He is with us always.

Another theme of the book is that the true source of life comes from God and not this world. We cannot know how to live life well in this world if we do not first find real life in fellowship with God through prayer and service. Therefore, Thomas challenges our perspectives about things; always pointing out how we need to have an eternal perspective regarding life's ups and downs, joys and sorrows, victories and defeats. Above all, Thomas challenges us to surrender all of our self to the loving will of God and receive all of Jesus in return. Only when we "let go and let God" can we truly live the abundant life that Jesus taught. Only when we stop trying to get what we can for ourselves can we start loving our neighbor. Only when we stop trying to love for our own glory can we truly bring glory to God. *The Imitation of Christ* not only reminds us to love God and neighbor, it is also very practical in teaching us how to do that in our daily walk with God.

In *Beyond Self*, Jason Rowinski has updated and paraphrased Books I and II from *The Imitation of Christ*. As you read this updated part of a great spiritual classic, remember that God wants to do the same thing in you that He did in Thomas à Kempis. This doesn't necessarily mean that God wants you to write a great Christian devotional book, though that may be a possibility. It does mean that God wants to transform your ordinary life with His extraordinary love. God wants you to give Him your life so that He can give you Jesus' life in return. Like Thomas à Kempis and other saints who've gone before, you can also be one who imitates Christ.

A Note About This Book and the Series

This book is one in a series called "The Ancient Faith Series." The purpose of this series is to take some of the thoughts and writings of those who have traveled the Christian path before us and breathe new life into their words of wisdom; words that have stood the test of time. By updating the language, we can bring the heart and message of some of the great lessons of the faith into the present day.

With this book by Saint Thomas à Kempis, we have tried to stay as true to the aim and intention of the original writer as possible. Throughout the book we have done whatever we could to bring to light the original meaning of the writer, but say it in today's language. It is our hope that we have been able to take the words of this ancient book and make them relevant in the present day.

Book 1
The Basics of the Spiritual Life

1 Living Beyond Self means recognizing the emptiness of this world

Jesus said, "*Whoever follows me will never walk in darkness*" (John 8:12). These simple words teach you to imitate His life and character. Living Christ's life must be the focus of your life if you want to have an amazing relationship with God. Living in the light means you're free from spiritual blindness.

The good news of Jesus Christ is higher than all human understanding, religious and otherwise. Those who follow the leading of the Holy Spirit learn this and discover the *true* Bread of Life. Sadly, many hear the good news taught by Jesus, but it doesn't change them. They choose not to walk by the guidance of the Holy Spirit. It doesn't have to be this way! You can know deeply in your heart the living words of Christ. This kind of knowing comes from choosing to mold your life completely and uncompromisingly to the life of Christ. Keep in mind that a deep spiritual life doesn't come through head knowledge alone. What good is it to you, or anyone else, if you can debate the beliefs about the Trinity and yet you are not a humble person? Lack of humility is displeasing to the Triune God. Big words and spiritual arguments do not make you right with God. Love and obedience please God. True spiritual conviction is more important than understanding the definition of a big religious word. Knowing the whole Bible by heart and understanding the teachings of world-renowned philosophers mean nothing if you don't truly know the love of God and live a grace-filled life.

You must believe that the Christ-filled life is the only real life. It is a selfish waste of time to seek the world's recognition, the affirmation of people, and positions of influence. It's a selfish waste of time to focus your thoughts and plans on how to please your sinful desires. Besides, you'll only suffer from guilt and its consequences by doing this. It's a selfish waste of time to worry about living a long life when you have no clue how to live an abundant life. It's a selfish waste of time to worry only about what is going on in your life right now without having a greater vision of what God wants to do in and through your life. It's a selfish waste of time to desire anything that is not part of God's purpose for you, whether it is a person, a plan, or a possession. These things are only temporary.

Be eager to love those things that are part of God's purpose, because that is where you'll find everlasting joy! As often as you need to—daily, hourly, or every minute—remind yourself of this truth: "*The eye never has enough of seeing, nor the ear its fill of hearing*" (Ecclesiastes 1:8). The things of this world only make you happy for a moment. If you try to find lasting happiness in them, you'll end up empty and craving more—like an addict. Quit trying to make the visible things of this world meet your need. Turn to the invisible reality of God's gracious care, which is more real than what your five senses (taste, touch, smell, hearing, and sight) tell you. Those who try to please their five senses alone end up trying to please themselves, but this stains their conscience and loses God's favor.

2 Living Beyond Self means keeping a humble perspective about yourself

It's natural for humans to desire knowledge. But what good is knowledge if you aren't in awe of God's knowledge? A humble farmer that serves God is better off than a proud thinker who neglects his or her own soul in order to become an expert scholar. The person who knows himself or herself well grows in humility and doesn't seek the praise of other people for his or her identity. If you know all things in the world but do not understand how to love selflessly, what good will that do you when you stand before God—the One who will judge you by what you have done with your knowledge. Turn away from the pursuit of getting knowledge for its own sake. This will sidetrack you from what is most important and make you a prideful person. Many scholars love degrees, awards, and to be sought out as experts. There is a lot you can learn which is of little use to your spiritual life. It's unwise to pursue these things with more passion and interest than you do your relationship with God. New ideas alone will not satisfy your soul. Only a good life brings peace of mind and a clean conscience and assures you of peace with God.

Holy people understand this truth: the greater the knowledge, the greater the responsibility and more severe the judgment for not obeying what they know to be true. Therefore, don't be proud because of your learning or abilities. Your learning and abilities should make you more humble and careful in all you do. If you think that you are intelligent and capable, remember there's still a lot that you don't know. So don't pretend you are more important or intelligent than you actually are; rather, admit your own limitations. It makes no sense to prefer your own insight to that of mature Christians, people who are wiser and more experienced than you are. The person who really wants to learn something worthwhile must let go of the need for others' approval.

The way of growth and learning begins with viewing yourself honestly. Perfect wisdom comes from thinking more highly of others than you do of yourself. Don't pat yourself on the back and think that you're great when you see someone else sin or make a huge mistake. You don't know how long it will be before you are in their place, in need of grace. Every person has some weakness, but you ought to think of yourself as the weakest of all.

3 Living Beyond Self means walking the path of truth

Happy is the person who lives by the truth when he or she hears it and avoids the shallowness of this world. We often follow blindly our opinions and senses, but they confuse and deceive us more than they help. What good is endless discussion about obscure matters when they won't matter to God on Judgment Day? It's unwise to neglect things that are good and wise to pursue things that are harmful and irrelevant. We have eyes but refuse to see the truth!

Why are we so concerned with scientific reasoning and philosophical concepts in our search for the meaning of life? When the Word of God speaks to you, it sets you free from such fruitless searching. All things come from the one Eternal WORD—the beginning of all knowledge. It is awesome to know that He speaks to us personally! Without that Word speaking to us, we won't know or do what is right. But when you see everything through the perspective of the Word, your mind will be at peace and you will be able to rest in God. *Oh, God the Truth—make me one with You in everlasting love! I'm often tired and empty after reading or hearing the words of this world. You're all I want and need. Let the wise be still and creation be silent before You so I can hear Your voice alone!*

The more inner integrity a person possesses and the simpler and pure his or her heart, the easier it is for this person to understand things because light from heaven shines in his or her mind. A pure, simple, and faithful-spirited person is not distracted even when he or she is busy because all this person does is in service to God. A person like this is at peace, so no selfish goal is sought.

Nothing gives a person more trouble and stress than desires of the heart not given fully to God. A good and godly person inwardly sets his or her mind on what is right, and then does it. This person does not allow uncontrolled selfishness to take him or her down the wrong path. This person chooses to act according to a mind fixed on God. No one faces a greater battle than the battle to overcome selfishness. Our goal ought to be to conquer selfishness, becoming stronger each day by yielding more and more of ourselves to God. All so-called human perfection mixes with imperfection. Human understanding is limited and not without some misunderstanding. That's why humble self-awareness is a more dependable way to grow closer to God than an ambitious pursuit of knowledge.

Let me be very clear: learning is not evil and knowledge is not useless! These things are good because they are some of God's gifts for people. The problem is that humans make them more important than God by worshiping them. That's why we should first give our energy to having a pure conscience and living an honest life. People often get this backwards and make knowledge more important than living well. That's why they are so confused, unproductive, and unhappy in life.

If people spent as much time rooting out selfishness and planting seeds of love as they do worrying about learning and success, there wouldn't be nearly as much evil and scandal in the world or as much complacency and weakness in the Church. The truth is that on Judgment Day God won't ask us about what we've read, but what we've done. He won't care about how profound our speeches were but how well we lived.

Tell me, where are all the past famous teachers and authors now? While they lived, people followed them faithfully. Now that they're dead, new ones have quickly risen up in their places. In their lifetime they seemed so important, but now they are just an afterthought. How quickly the glory of the world passes away! If only their lives were as good as their understanding, then all their intellectual efforts might truly have been worthwhile.

There are so many who perish because they pursue the things of this world but care little about serving God. These types choose popularity over humility and end up lost in their own sense of self-importance. The truth is that the one who loves selflessly is truly great. The one who doesn't seek the spotlight is truly great. The one who doesn't seek to find his or her identity in this world but finds it in Christ is truly wise. The one who does God's will and not his or her own will is truly knowledgeable.

4 Living Beyond Self means thinking about what you do before you do it

Be careful not to listen to every suggestion of others or every one of your impulses. Think before you act. Carefully and patiently consider things in light of God's will. It's because people are weak spiritually, emotionally, and mentally that they find it easier to believe and speak evil of others (rather than good). People perfected by God's love and spiritual discipline do not jump to conclusions for they know that most humans are weak and prone to evil. You see this kind of weakness in others by the way they speak.

You demonstrate great wisdom by not making quick decisions or clinging stubbornly to your own opinion. You also demonstrate great wisdom when you choose not to believe everything you hear about others or spread gossip and rumors. Figure out what is true and what comes from God by seeking direction from spiritually sensitive and wise Christians. You're much better off seeking the advice of spiritually mature people and following it rather than following what *you* think is right. A person who lives this way lives a good life—a life of godly wisdom which can be applied to all situations. The more humble and determined to follow God's lead a person is, the more effective that person will be in life and blessed with a continuous sense of inner peace and joy.

5 Living Beyond Self means meditating on the Bible

Read the Bible, looking for the truth behind the words. Do not just to memorize the verses so that you can show others that you're smart. You must choose to read each part of the Bible with the Holy Spirit's inspiration because the Holy Spirit inspired the original authors of the Bible. Determine to read the Bible with the purpose of spiritual growth. Do not focus on mastering the information, but focus on it changing your heart. This attitude must carry over into everything that you read, which is good for your spiritual life be it simple or profound. The love of truth should be your motivation for reading a book, not the author's level of education or popularity. Pay more attention to what is taught than the reputation or skill of the teacher.

Human teachers come and go but God's truth lasts forever. God doesn't pick favorites. He speaks to us all, and all can know His truth. Sometimes one can get too caught up in debating technical questions while missing the truth entirely. To understand the Bible deeply, you must begin with the attitude of your heart. Read with humility, openness, and faithfulness. Don't worry about being considered an expert. Consider the words, written by holy people who've come before you, with a willing heart and a quiet mind. Pay attention to what they say and obey them.

6 Living Beyond Self means balancing your desires

You can tell your desires are out of order when you have a restless and anxious spirit. People who want things their own way are never at peace. Only those who let go of their own agenda and trust God live in peace. If you do not die to yourself daily, you'll be tempted and overcome by many trivial things. The spiritually immature person who is still controlled by his or her senses, instincts, and personal agendas has little chance of overcoming selfish desires. When this person tries to get free from them, he or she discovers a lot of inner conflict. When someone or something stands in the way of a person getting what he or she wants, this person may get frustrated and angry.

If that person continues going his or her own way, he or she will not have true peace of mind because God will convict him or her. Deep down inside this person knows it is wrong to give in to his or her own will (even though in the end, it makes no sense to follow your own will because you never end up with the peace you seek). Resist these selfish desires; don't give in to them and you'll find peace. Real peace doesn't come to a selfish person, or a person addicted to people or possessions. Real peace only comes to those who pursue God with passion.

7 Living Beyond Self means eliminating false hope and pride

You give yourself false hope if you put your trust in people or things. Don't be ashamed to serve others for the love of Jesus Christ and don't be ashamed if you don't measure up to the world's standards of wealth and success. Place your trust in God, not in your abilities or popularity. Choose to do the good that you have the power to do and God will help you. Don't allow your own thinking or the smooth words of others to guide your way. Rely upon the grace of God who helps the humble and humbles the proud.

If you are wealthy and have many powerful and influential friends, don't take a lot satisfaction from it. It's God who gives everything, and the most important gift He gives is himself. Don't take pride in your personal stature or physical beauty, these things don't last long and you can lose them simply by getting sick. Don't take pride in your ability or talents because this displeases God—the One who gave you these gifts. Don't make the mistake of thinking of yourself better than others for only God knows what's in a person's heart. Don't think your good deeds alone impress God. Keep in mind that it is often the things that please others that displease God. See more good in others than you do in yourself for this will help you remain humble. It does no harm to you to think of yourself as less than others. It does great harm to you to think better of yourself than even one person. The humble live in continuous peace, while envy and frequent anger fill the hearts of the proud.

8 Living Beyond Self means choosing close friends wisely

Don't just open your heart up to anybody! It's better to discuss what's going on inside you with spiritually mature people who fear God. Be careful and wise about who you allow into your close circle of friends. Don't throw yourself at the rich or popular crowd. Your close friendship circle should consist of the humble and simple, the devout and virtuous; speak with them often and about things that build you up. It's dangerous to become too personal with an individual of the opposite sex whom you aren't married to, but there is nothing wrong with forming godly friendships with this person. Seek deep intimacy with God alone, and avoid shallow acquaintances.

Jesus calls you to love and serve all people, but not necessarily to be best friends with everyone. Sometimes a person has a good reputation with others; however, when you get to know this person you are not impressed by his or her character. Even with yourself, you may think others want to be around you when in truth you may annoy them by some of your words and actions.

9 Beyond Self means learning to be obedient

It is a great thing to live in obedience to God by trusting what your spiritual mentors tell you to do, and not just do what you think is right. It is much safer to walk in obedience yourself rather than instruct others how to do so. There are some people who obey, but not out of love for God. This doesn't work, and it's not what God wants! These people are easily frustrated and unhappy, mope around, and complain a lot. They can't find peace of mind because they obey only out of a sense of duty and fear, not because they wholeheartedly love God. Go ahead and try living life your own way, but I promise you won't find the abundant life until you humbly choose to come under the spiritual guidance of Christians who are more spiritually mature than you. Peoples' own imaginations and change of circumstances often lead them down the wrong path. These things can be very deceptive.

Know this: everyone wants to do what seems right to them and will hang out with others who agree with them and shut out the voices that don't. However, if God is truly with you, there are times when you'll discover that you need to give up your own ideas for the sake of peace. What person is so wise that they know everything? There is no such person. That's why you shouldn't trust your own ideas too much. A wise person listens to others. Even if you think your way is the right way, you can't go wrong by accepting the wise advice of another because you love God and are trying to be obedient. It's smarter to listen to advice and take it than it is to give it. It's possible that your way may be right. However, refusing to agree with others when reason and occasion demand it is a sign of pride and stubbornness.

10 Living Beyond Self means being careful with what we say

We should avoid talking too much about worldly affairs as often as possible. Even though we may be sincere, such idle debate often spirals downward, giving our prideful attitudes and actions opportunity to flourish. Many times I have spoken carelessly when I should have remained quiet and kept to myself. I wonder why it is that we are so eager to share our opinions and gossip with each other. Especially knowing that these conversations often result in feelings of conviction over what we said. I think the answer is that we seek the comfort of having other people agree with our opinion. This eases the strain placed on us by so many different voices in this world.

Comfort is also the reason why we are so eager to think and talk about the things that excite us the most, or the things that we really don't like.

Sadly, our thoughts and words often don't produce anything good. The enjoyment we get from always talking and thinking about ourselves often shuts God out and that's why we don't grow spiritually. It's critical, then, for us to pray often and avoid wasting valuable time and energy. Then when the right moment comes for speaking, we'll say something worthwhile. We speak carelessly because we don't have a deeper conversational relationship with God. If we really want to make solid spiritual progress, we should make it our practice to speak about important spiritual matters with mature Christians with whom we're unified in mind and spirit.

11 Living Beyond Self means living peacefully with a passion for spiritual growth

Our lives would be very peaceful if we weren't so worried about controlling what others say and do, for this is not our responsibility. How do we expect to remain in peace when we spend all your time focused on other people's issues—leaving little or no time to reflect on our own need for growth? People with simple trust are at peace.

Why do so few Christians discover perfect peace and a reflective life? It's because only a few have put to death their earthly desires, which enabled them to focus wholeheartedly on God, freeing them to reflect on their innermost selves. The problem for the rest of us is our obsession with our own passions and seeking happiness in things that will pass away. This is why it's rare for us to overcome even one sin in our lives and not be passionate about improving ourselves everyday. Instead, we just remain cold and indifferent.

If we died to selfishness every day and stopped trying to secure happiness apart from God, we would see and appreciate God's abundant presence and activity in our lives, which is like tasting some of heaven now. Our greatest, indeed our only obstacle, is that we are not free from the passions and lusts of this life. We neglect the perfect way of life discovered by the mature Christians who have gone before us. Slight difficulties in life throw us completely off track, and then we go and make our situation worse by trying to take refuge in human comforts.

Only by standing bravely in the face of this battle, instead of running away, can we discover how much God himself is assisting us! God often gives us the opportunity to fight so that we can emerge victorious. He is ready to help those who fight to the end and trust in His grace. We cannot let our spiritual progress be defined by religious behavior alone or we won't be devoted to God very long. We must chop down the root of our sin so that we may be freed from our passions and find God's lasting peace. For example, if we would concentrate on rooting out one barrier to our spiritual growth each year we'd be well along the path of perfect love.

Sadly, many do the exact opposite. Many discover they were more peaceful, purer, and passionate when they first became Christians than after many years of practicing the faith. It should be the case that our passion for, and growth in, Christ increases every day. Today people are surprised if a person keeps even a small part of his or her initial passion for Jesus! If we would just take things a little more seriously at the beginning of our commitments to Christ, then all growth in grace after that would come much easier and more joyful.

It's hard to break old habits and it's even harder to go against our own will. If we don't overcome the insignificant things we won't be able to overcome more difficult issues. Resist selfishness when it begins and unlearn your sinful habits, or these will slowly pull you downward into even greater difficulties. We should imagine having a peaceful life and bringing joy to others! In turn, this might make us more focused in our spiritual life!

12 Living Beyond Self means turning adversity into advantage

Sometimes it is good for us to have troubles and trials, for they have a way of causing us to slow down and reflect on the temporary nature of life. That's when we realize that it's not good to trust too much in worldly things. Sometimes it is good for us to have people that oppose us, misjudge us, or bear us ill will—even though we mean well and do good. Such opposition is humbling and defends us from the need to be approved by everyone. For when people do not think well of us and give us no credit, we are more inclined to seek God's affirmation alone.

Therefore, a person ought to only depend on his or her standing with God and not seek the approval of other people. When good people are afflicted, tempted, or assaulted with evil thoughts, they must clearly understand how much they need God to overcome them—for without Him they can do nothing good. Faced with this suffering, good people are sorrowful and pray and repent. They desire to be with Christ. It is only then that they come to know a very important spiritual truth: *perfect security and total peace cannot be found in anything in this world.*

13 Living Beyond Self means resisting temptation

Suffering and temptation are a fact of this life. The Book of Job says "*Human life is a struggle*" (7:1, TM). It is important for us to pay attention and pray so we can understand our temptations and do not let the devil find ways to deceive us. The enemy never sleeps, but goes about seeking someone to devour. No one is so perfect or holy that they are above temptations; in this world no one is free from them. Even though temptations are frustrating and dangerous, they can be useful to us as opportunities to be humbled, purified, and instructed by the Holy Spirit. All the saints passed through many trials and temptations and grew spiritually through patience during these times. Those who could not wait patiently on God became rebellious and turned away from Him.

I cannot stress this point enough. There is no level of

spiritual maturity we can reach or secret place where we can find temptations and trials will not come. No one is free from temptation in this life. We were born with an inclination to evil and that sinful nature gives power to these temptations. Humanity fell far away from its original state of innocence and all creation is affected by sin. When one temptation or trial goes away another takes its place.

Many people try to escape or ignore temptations, but this only causes them to fail more seriously down the road. We cannot overcome temptations by running away from them. We overcome our enemies through the spiritual strength developed by the daily practice of patience and humility. Some learn to avoid temptations through rigid discipline, but they don't deal with the root of temptation. They make little or no progress spiritually, and the temptations they "avoided" return quickly and stronger than ever. Little by little, through patience and obedience, and with God's help, you will overcome temptations. This is much healthier than punishing ourselves or contriving some ill-advised scheme of dealing with temptations. Seek wise counsel when tempted. We shouldn't be hard on others who are tempted, but rather, should give comfort and guidance to them in the same way we would want someone to comfort and guide us.

All temptations begin with a wavering mind that has little trust in God. Such a weak minded and faithless person is tempted in many ways. Like a ship in a storm without a rudder, he or she is tossed about by the waves of temptation. As fire tempers iron, so temptation strengthens the just person. Sometimes we aren't sure of what we're capable of and then a battle with temptation shows us our strength. We must always remain alert, especially in the beginning of temptation. It is much easier to overcome the enemy if we don't open the door of our hearts to him. We must resist him at the door when he first knocks. A wise person once said, "It's better to resist evil when it begins rather than try to figure out how to deal with it later, because it is often too late."

First, it begins with a small thought. Second, we give life to that thought with our imagination. Third, we take pleasure in that thought. Fourth, we develop an evil scheme to obtain what we want. Finally, we choose to go after it. This is the path from temptation to sin. This is how Satan gains full entry in to our minds . . . we did not resist him in the beginning. The longer a person delays in resisting, the weaker he or she becomes each day, while the strength of the enemy grows against him or her.

We should not get discouraged when faced with temptations, but rather, should seek God more eagerly. During these times we must ask God to give us strength, guidance, and direction each step of the way. Remember the words of Paul: "*with . . . temptation [God] will provide the way of escape . . . , so that you will be able to endure it*" (1 Corinthians 10:13, NASB). At each temptation we must throw ourselves before God—the One who promises to help us overcome and resist all the enemy throws in our path.

14 Living Beyond Self means not rushing to judgment

We should be more concerned with ourselves than we are about with what everyone else is doing. Judging others is ineffective because we are often mistaken, or worse, our judgments easily cause us to stumble. On the flip side, honest and penetrating self-examination is always fruitful. We think our judgments are correct, but the truth is our feelings often get in the way of our seeing clearly. If God were truly all we wanted or needed, we wouldn't get so frustrated at opposition to our opinions or be so demanding that others agree with us.

Yet, we're easily drawn down the wrong path, usually by a desire inside us or by something that we have experienced. Many of us seek to satisfy our selfishness in what we do without being aware of what we're doing. When things are going well we look peaceful. However, when things don't go according to our plans, we get confused and upset. This is how simple differences often end up dividing people, even committed Christians.

Old habits are hard to break and most of us are not willing to be led farther than we can see. If we rely more upon our own reasoning than we rely upon the Holy Spirit's ability to help us be more like Jesus Christ, it will be a long time before we truly mature in faith (if ever). God wants us to trust Him by completely submitting ourselves to Him and, through His passionate love, rise above our imperfect and limited human reasoning.

15 Beyond Self means that love for others is your main motivation

There is no good reason at all for you to do evil, nor should you do evil because of your love for another person. There are times when it is best for you not to step in and help someone, but wait until a greater good can happen in his or her life. You are not wrong in delaying doing a good act when you are being patient and preparing to act when the time is best. Without a selfless and sacrificial love, what you do has no lasting value. Whatever you do selflessly and sacrificially, even when it seems small and trivial in the eyes of the world, is very fruitful and good in God's eyes. God cares more about the quality of love in your heart than He does about your deeds. The person who loves much does much good.

The person who does something with excellence does much good. The person who serves others rather than his or her own interests also does much good. Beware, though, because sometimes what you think is sacrificial love is really self-love. This is because a person's self-centered nature, desires, hope of reward, and self-interest are seldom absent from his or her motivation.

The person that has true and perfect love seeks self in nothing, but desires only the glory of God in all things. This person envies no one because he or she seeks no personal gratification. This person does not wish to be celebrated. This person rejoices in seeing God glorified above all things. This person believes that good things don't come from people, but from the God who is the fountain of all good. Those who truly live the blessed life rest in God as their highest fulfillment. If people only had but one spark of this true and perfect love within them, they would see that all the things of this world are empty and unfulfilling!

16 Living Beyond Self means being patient with other people's imperfections

While God helps us grow spiritually, be patient with the imperfections we find in ourselves and others. We need to see such trials as opportunities to grow in godly patience. If we don't develop a godly, patient character, all of our good works are rather useless. When we face such difficulties, we need to pray that God will be with us and help us bear them calmly. If we've given serious spiritual guidance to a person once or twice and he or she refuses to listen, don't try to hassle this person into doing the right thing. We need to prayerfully commit such a person to God, trusting that His will to be done and His name honored in all His servants. God alone knows how to draw good from evil. We should also be patient with the defects and ignorance of others, whatever they are, because we ourselves have many faults that others must put up with. If we struggle with being the person we should be, how is it fair that we expect another person to have it all together? We may expect others to be perfect, but are less passionate about correcting our own faults. We may want to see others get their act together, but stubbornly refuse to be corrected ourselves. We may get upset that others live according to their own desires and yet we get upset when we don't get what *we* want. We may like others to obey rules and regulations; however we desire that no restraints be placed on us. Truthfully, we judge our neighbors harder than we would want others to judge us.

If everyone were perfect, how would we learn to love them as they are, as God loves them, or love them simply because we love God? God desires that we learn to love one another despite our faults. There is no person on earth without fault or without burden. Not one person is self-sufficient or wise enough on his or her own. We need each other! We need each other for support, comfort, encouragement, guidance, and accountability. We discover how strong and mature we are through adversity. Adversity does not weaken a person; rather it reveals whether or not they are truly strong and mature.

17 Living Beyond Self means living the life of a servant

If you want to live in peace and unity with others, you must learn to break your stubborn will. Living as a Christian, whether alone or in a community of believers, without complaint and with life-long faithfulness is a big accomplishment. People who have experienced true Christian community are blessed. You can die happy and content knowing that you have lived well. If you want to continue to grow in grace, you must consider yourself a stranger in this world, a pilgrim on the way to a better place. If you want to be like Jesus Christ, you must be content with the fact that many people won't understand your way of life.

Outward changes and rules, such as wearing different clothes than the world, do little to make you different. Changing your worldview and your attitudes and dying to self are the things that make a person truly different. If you seek anything but God alone and the salvation of your soul, you will only discover trouble and grief. If you do not make it your goal to give up your power and privileges and become the servant of all, your peace won't last.

God asks Christians to serve, not rule. A servant makes sacrifices, works with passion, and doesn't waste precious time with gossip or laziness. The choice to be a servant refines a person like gold in a furnace. It is impossible to stay committed to the life of a servant unless you choose, wholeheartedly and lovingly, to surrender your life to God.

18 Living Beyond Self means following the footsteps of the Christian saints before us

Think of all the Christian saints that came before us who are shining examples of perfect love and passion for God. By comparison, we do very little, almost nothing, these days. What would our lives amount to compared to them? The saints and friends of Christ served the Lord in hunger and thirst, in cold and nakedness, in work and fatigue, in vigils and fasts, in prayer and meditation, and in many persecutions and accusations. The apostles, martyrs, confessors, and all the rest suffered very much because they followed in the footsteps of Christ! They turned away from the comforts of life because they were set on living this life with an eternal perspective.

Reflect on the lives of the holy desert hermits. They lived strict and self-denying lives; suffered long and serious temptations; endured the enemy's continual assaults; offered frequent and fervent prayers to God; fasted seriously; pursued spiritual growth with passion and love; fought bravely to master their evil desires; and maintained pure and honest love for God! They worked hard during the day and then spent long hours at night praying.

When they were working, their minds were still focused on God in prayer. They used their time well, devoting every hour to serving God. Sometimes when they got caught up with God in prayer, they forgot their own bodily needs. They renounced all riches, dignities, honors, friends, and family, for they chose not to have any comfort in this world. They scarcely allowed themselves life's necessities and only took care of their body when necessary—and even this bothered them. They were poor by the world's standards. Yet, they were rich in grace and virtue, outwardly destitute and inwardly full of the gracious presence of God. Strangers to this world, they were intimate friends of God. They didn't think highly of themselves and were despised by the world. Yet in God's eyes, they were precious and beloved. They lived in true humility and simple obedience, walked in loving-kindness and patience, made daily progress on the spiritual path, and obtained great favor with God.

These people are examples for the faithful and should motivate us to pursue Christian maturity. Let's stop following the many examples of lukewarm Christians that tempt us with mediocrity. Think about the great love and passion in the Christian saints from the very beginning of their holy calling. Greatly devoted to prayer and pursuit of the good, they lived disciplined lives. When their spiritual mentors gave guidance, they accepted it with humility and obedience. The footsteps they left behind for us to see give witness to the fact that they truly were spiritual giants of holiness and maturity.

We must continue on the path walked by these faithful followers of Christ—those who fought bravely and emerged victorious over the world. It's so sad how far we've fallen from their examples! Some people have lowered their standards so far that they consider those who simply avoid sin and quietly accept their daily duties as spiritual giants and examples. How lukewarm and negligent! Many lose their original passion quickly and come to a place where their own laziness and apathy has made them weary of life! How can anyone be OK with being spiritually immature when we have so many examples of devout Christians? I pray to God that we gain more desire and passion to grow in His grace.

19 Living Beyond Self means exercising your faith

Faithful Christians must be people with good character. They should have integrity, being the same on the inside as they claim to be on the outside. Actually, there should be much more substance on the inside than what is seen on the outside. God sees all—inside and out. You ought to worship Him despite the circumstances. No matter where you are, you must always show respect toward God in all you say and do. Each day you need to renew your purposes and to build up your passion for Christ as though it were the first day you became a Christian. Each day you should say, "*Help me, my God, as I endeavor to serve You and fulfill Your **purposes** for me. It is a brand new day and I desire a perfect beginning, for everything I've done up to this point is now in the past and today is a fresh start.*"

You should work to achieve the goals you set for your life. If you want each day to be a good day with God, you must pay close attention to that objective. If it is true that even the strong-willed person can fail, then what about a person who scarcely makes up his or her mind and only does things half-heartedly? Many things can keep you from fulfilling our spiritual goals and objectives. Even getting a little off track with your spiritual disciplines (practices that bring you closer to God such as praying, reading the Bible, fasting, and so on) can bring negative results. Righteous people depend on the grace of God, not their own will power, in staying focused on being a faithful follower. Before they do anything, they bring it to

God in prayer. The ability to fulfill your spiritual goals comes from Him alone. God's way, not yours, is always the right way.

If there is a legitimate reason why you missed your normal routine of spiritual disciplines, like a greater spiritual act or because of ministering to another person, don't stress over it; just pick up your spiritual routine the next day. But if your spiritual disciplines are a mess because of laziness or apathy, this hinders your spiritual growth. The truth is that even when trying hard, you will still fail in many things. This is no excuse. You still need a focused purpose, especially in combating your greatest weaknesses.

Your outward and inward lives must be watched closely and ordered carefully, for both are important to the Christlike life. If you can't continuously and prayerfully examine yourself, do it periodically, at least once a day. The best times are in the morning or in the evening. In the morning you can fix your mind on God's purposes and in the evening you can reflect on how you did in the way you talked, acted, and thought. You have to learn to face the day like a warrior preparing for battle against your enemy. Focus your heart on God and you will more easily master every desire of the flesh. Use your free time wisely, never allowing yourself to be completely idle. Read, write, pray, meditate, or do something good for someone else.

Be prayerful and careful when attempting to strengthen your spiritual life through spiritual disciplines. Not everyone is called to pray, fast, and so on in the same way. In fact, some acts of devotion are private and shouldn't be made public (personal prayer and Bible reading).

Such personal things are best kept between you, God, and possibly your spiritual leaders. At the same time you should also beware not to neglect the public and common acts of worship because of your own private devotions. However, if you have spare time after faithfully completing all that you normally should do as a Christian believer, feel free to focus on other personal acts of devotion.

Not everyone is called to the same devotional life, so pay attention to your particular calling, personality, and circumstances. Some devotional practices fit while others may not. Different devotional practices are suited for different times, some are good for special holy days and others are good for the regular workday. In times of temptation and questioning, you need certain types of devotions and disciplines. In times of peace and certainty, you need other devotions and disciplines. Some are suitable when you are sad and others when you are joyful. Having devotions and disciplines is necessary, but there is freedom to tailor them to your specific situation.

Practice group devotional exercises and intercessory prayer with other mature Christians, especially around the important times in the Christian year like Advent, Christmas, Lent, Easter, and Pentecost. From one special season to another, you ought to practice your devotions with the mindset that you will soon pass from this world and come to the everlasting feast day of king Jesus. These holy seasons are opportunities to refocus your life to holier living, more dependency on God's grace, and less on the things of this world. This is the best way to receive blessings from the hand of God.

If you don't continue to grow in grace through your devotions and disciplines, you should fully understand that you are not living life as God meant for you to live and you are incapable of the great glory that God desires to reveal in you when you're ready to receive it. Living right is also the best preparation for death. Remember what Luke's gospel quotes Jesus as saying: "*It will be good for those servants whose master finds them watching when he comes*" (12:37).

20 Living Beyond Self means learning to love solitude and silence

Find a time that's good for you so you can get away and reflect on God's loving-kindness. Don't fill this time with books for entertainment or education. Instead, use this time to read such things that bring conviction to your heart. If you withdraw yourself from unnecessary conversations, from listening to gossip and rumors, you'll find enough time that is suitable to reflect on good things. Many of the great saints withdrew purposefully from the casual company of people whenever possible in order to serve God through personal prayer. One writer even said, "*As often as I have been among people, I returned home feeling less a whole person than before.*" A person often finds this true after a long and unnecessary conversation. It's easier to be silent altogether than to keep yourself from speaking too much. It's easier to stay at home than always being on guard while out in your community. Anyone who aims to live the inner and spiritual life like Jesus must separate themselves from the crowd for times of solitude. No one can navigate the demands of other people unless he or she is first comfortable alone at home. No one is ready for public speaking until he or she has first learned to willingly hold his or her peace. No one should be a leader if he or she hasn't first learned to follow. No one should give direction unless he or she has learned well how to be obedient. No one should rejoice unless he or she has the inner confidence of a good conscience.

The saints maintained a healthy fear of the Lord and felt secure because of it. They became strong Christians because they refused to get complacent and were determined to grow in their faith. On the other hand, the security of the wicked comes from pride and arrogance. They deceive themselves about their true state of being. You should never get too comfortable with yourself in this life, even if you are a serious Christian! All too often it happens that those who've been looked up to by others fail in their spiritual lives because they mistakenly thought they were beyond sin. You are never beyond temptation, so you should always be conscious of all that surrounds you. If you don't do this, you will feel safe from sin, become filled with pride, and then be susceptible to easy failure. Stop seeking temporary highs or entangling yourself with worldly needs and you'll have a good conscience! Great peace and stability comes from cutting out unnecessary anxiety and setting the mind on divine things. You should focus your minds on things helpful to the soul and putting all trust in God.

You cannot find heaven's peace until you take sin and

the need for God seriously. Seek a private place and shut out the noise of the world. It is written, "In your private place be grieved over your sins." In solitude, you will find the peace and focus you cannot get in public. Your private place will become precious to you if you learn to spend time there. If you don't, you won't enjoy it at all. Learn the value of solitude at the beginning of your Christian journey and keep it as a regular spiritual discipline. If you do, you'll see how important it is to your spiritual health and will enjoy your time of privacy.

In silence and solitude, the devout soul grows in grace and learns the deeper truth of Scripture. There you'll find a flood of tears with which to bathe and cleanse yourself with nightly. You'll be intimately familiar with the Creator because you've withdrawn from the insanity of the world. If you stop filling all of your time up with friends and acquaintances, you'll make time for God and His holy angels will draw near to you. It's more important to tend to your own soul and salvation than to neglect it by trying to become important in this life. It's good for you if you don't need the attention of others, need to be entertained, or need to be busy all the time.

Why do you want to tempt yourself with things that aren't good for you anyway? The world is passing away, why lust for it? Your sensual desires sometimes entice you to find something outside to fulfill them. When you give into them, what do you bring back with you except a guilty conscience and a heavy heart? Carelessly going out often leads to a sad return, a merry evening to a mournful dawn. So it is with all carnal, worldly pleasures.

They begin sweetly but end up bringing remorse and death. What true pleasure can you find elsewhere that you can't find in solitude?

Think about the heavens, the earth, and all the elements—the stuff of God's creation. What can you see anywhere under the sun that will last forever? Perhaps you think you'll find something that will satisfy you, but you cannot. Even if you could see everything that exists, it would still be an empty vision. Keep this in mind: you cannot hold on to anything of this world.

Lift your eyes up to heaven in prayer and ask God to forgive you for your sins and shortcomings. Leave empty things to the people with empty souls. Set yourself to the things God has commanded you to do. Close the door of self-centeredness and call upon Jesus, the One you love. Remain with Him in silence and solitude, for nowhere else will you find lasting peace. If you listen to unnecessary gossip, you will not be at peace.

21 Living Beyond Self means developing a spiritually sensitive heart

If you want to live Christ's life, respect God in everything you say and do. Be careful with your freedom. Discipline your five senses and your daily schedule. Don't waste your time with foolish things. Develop a spiritually sensitive heart that leads to a deeper relationship with God. A spiritually sensitive heart opens the door to many good things that sinfulness destroys. How can any person who thinks about the true reality of this life, and the many dangers to his or her soul, ever be perfectly joyful? Sometimes people are careless and don't think about the tragedy of sin in the world and so they laugh when they should be weeping. You are not truly free or joyful unless your freedom and joy are rooted in respect for God and a good conscience. A person who sets his or her mind on developing spiritual sensitivity is truly happy. Only a person who abandons all that defiles and burdens his or her conscience is truly happy.

Fight sinfulness full-force! Overcome bad habits with good habits. Focus your intensity on what you need to do to grow and not on worrying about what everyone else needs to do. You cannot and should not control other people. People will be gracious to you if you are gracious to them. Don't stick your nose into other people's business or get entangled in situations more complicated than you understand. Keep your eyes fixed on yourself and reprimand yourself instead of your friends. Why care if you are not popular? If you worry about what people think of you, you'll start doing the wrong things to gain their approval, and this is a serious matter. As a Christian, find joy in your identity as God's servant. It's safer for your soul to not have too much recognition from the world.

God offers divine approval and comfort, but some rarely experience it. This is because they've not developed spiritual sensitivity and have not rejected the pointlessness of this world's pursuits. Believe sincerely that you still need God's grace every day and that you deserve the consequences of your sin. This will bring you to godly sorrow, where this world's agenda is seen for what it really is—fallen. A good person always finds enough in life over which to be sorrowful. Think of your own troubles or those of the people closest to you and you will quickly see there is a lot of suffering around you. This reflection brings one to a real sense of grief. People's sins and vices entangle them so much that they can rarely apply themselves to the concerns of heaven, which would bring them to rightful sorrow and inner remorse.

One spiritual discipline that is very helpful for growth in spiritual sensitivity is thinking about the reality of death and then remembering that you determine now whether you'll go on living for eternity with God or dying eternally without Him. Thinking of life from this perspective will change the way you handle difficult situations as you will no longer fear any hardship in this world. Most people usually don't like to think about these things so they never pierce their hearts. They are captivated by the praises and pleasures of this world, so they remain cold and indifferent to God. They often complain about their frustrations with this life because they lack spiritual depth and peace. Pray humbly to the Lord then, that He will develop within you a spiritually sensitive heart. Then you can say with the prophet, *Feed me, Lord, "with the bread of tears" and give me to "drink tears by the bowlful"* (Psalm 80:5).

22 Living Beyond Self means understanding the true source of happiness

I guarantee you'll be miserable if you look to anyone or anything other than God as the source of your happiness. Why are you so troubled when things don't go your way? Who do you know that always gets what they want? The answer: no one! Even kings, presidents, and other leaders experience some trouble and confusion. Who has real happiness? People who are able to suffer something for God's glory are truly happy. Many hurting and struggling people think, "Look at so-and-so's life! They have everything—wealth, good looks, power, and fame." But if they would only lift up their eyes a little higher toward heaven they'd see that all the wealth of this life doesn't amount to much. The people you think have everything are uncertain and become burdens to others because they are never without anxiety and fear.

Human happiness never comes from having a lot of stuff; a moderate amount of things should be enough. Living life is enough of a challenge without adding concerns for stuff to the mix. People who grow spiritually become less and less consumed with getting stuff in this life. They see more clearly and are more sensitive to the defects of human corruption. Thinking only about life's basics like eating and drinking, sleeping and thinking, working and resting, as well as the worrying about the other necessities of nature, is a great burden and frustration to the spiritual person—who would gladly let go of the sinfulness in this world and just live in simplicity.

The inner soul gets weighed down by outward human necessities. That's why the prophet prayed with great devotion, "*free me from my anguish*" (Psalm 25:17). People who aren't in touch with their own misery should be warned. A greater warning should be issued to those that are in love with this miserable and corrupt life! There are some people who are totally concerned about this life alone. Yet their entire fixation barely gets them the things they need to stay alive. They act like they would choose to live here forever and care nothing at all for the kingdom of God. This is evidence of a senseless and unbelieving heart. These people, so deeply committed to the ways of this world, can only enjoy worldly things! Miserable as they are now, in the end it will be far worse for them when they discover how they've only pursued empty things. On the other hand, the saints of God and friends of Christ didn't care too much for the things that pleased the flesh, or the things that were important in this life, but longed for heavenly riches with all their hearts. They focused their entire lives on the lasting, but unseen, things of God. Their need for the temporary and visible things of this world grew small.

Brothers and sisters, don't give up hope of making progress in godliness; it's not too late! Why would you keep putting it off? Get up now and say: "Now is the time to be doing, now is the time to be striving, and now is the time to get right with God." The best time to do the right thing by God is when you are confused and anxious! Everyone must pass through fire and water before they come to a place of spiritual rest. In this life, there will always be obstacles to spiritual growth. Unless you commit your whole self to growth, you will never find freedom from sin's reign in your life. Sin, weariness, and pain are always going to be a part of this life. It would be nice if everyone could be free from them, but it's precisely because of sin that people have lost their innocence. Therefore, you must learn patience and how to wait on the mercy of God until the difficult times pass. You must live this way in a fallen world.

O how great is human brokenness; it's always prone to evil! People confess their sins today, and then turn around and sin exactly the same way the next day! People say that they are going to change, and do for a moment, but soon behave in such a way that you would never guess they made a decision to change in the first place! You should humble yourself and never again be prideful, since people can be so weak and inconsistent. Besides, whatever you quickly gain by the grace of God can be quickly lost by your own negligence.

What will become of you in the end if early on your choice to follow God becomes lukewarm? You need to be warned not to rest easily in peace and safety especially before you're spiritually mature! You need to be instructed again, like beginners, in the nature of the true "good life" if you have any hope of some future change and spiritual maturity.

23 Living Beyond Self means having no fear of death

Since your death will come sooner than you think, you should seriously consider where you are going to spend eternity. Life is fragile. One day you're here, the next you're gone. When you're out of sight, it's not too long before you're also out of others' minds. It is silly and hard-hearted to think only about the present and not care about the future! Live with the end in mind. Order your thoughts and life as if you were about to die. If you have a good conscience, you won't fear death as much. Focus on avoiding sin, not dodging death! If you aren't prepared to die today, what makes you think you will be prepared tomorrow? Tomorrow is uncertain! You don't know that you'll be alive tomorrow.

What good is it to you to have a long life if you aren't becoming more like Jesus? Sadly, living long usually adds to your sinfulness, not your holiness. Oh that people would spend at least one day in this world living as God intended! There are many people who can tell you how long they have been Christians but you wouldn't know it because their lives are unfruitful. If you consider dying dreadful, consider that living is more dangerous. You will be at peace at the hour of your death if you prepared daily for it. When someone dies, be aware that it will one day be you.

Here's how this spiritual practice works. When it's morning, thank God for the gift of life and ask Him to prepare you for whatever comes your way. When night comes, and you're still alive, thank Him for another day of life. Whether it is morning or evening, don't allow yourself to think tomorrow is guaranteed. This way you will be in a constant state of readiness, leading life in such a way that death will never surprise you. Some people die suddenly. This should make you think about what Jesus said, "*The Son of Man will come at an hour when you do not expect him*" (Matthew 24:44).

When that last hour comes, you will begin to have a far different opinion of your life and will be sorry if you've been careless and purposeless. The wise person is the one that strives to live life *now* as God intends it to be lived! This person will have no regrets on his or her deathbed. Such a person renounces allegiance to this world, has a fervent passion to grow spiritually, and practices the hard work of repentance. This person is totally obedient to God, denies himself or herself, and bears life's troubles patiently because of his or her love for Christ. This person will die happy. It's easy to do good when you are healthy, but harder when you're sick. Few people grow spiritually during such times in their lives, just as purposeless people don't become holy.

Don't become lazy by resting on the faith of your friends and family. You're responsible for your own soul. Human beings have short memories. They will forget you sooner than you think. It's better to prepare yourself for death than to leave things to chance or hope others will come to the rescue. If you don't take care of yourself now, who will care for you later? The present time is precious. Today is the day of salvation. *Now* is the best time.

It's so sad to think that anyone would just waste time here when they might truly be living the life that will prepare them for eternity. If you aren't ready for eternity, the time will come when you'll wish you had the time to make amends to God and others. I can't guarantee that you'll get it. Beloved friend, think about the great dangers in life you're avoiding and the fear of death you'll no longer have if you only prepare prayerfully for it now! Work to get to the place in your heart where, when you are at the hour of death, you'll rejoice rather than fear. Learn now to die to the world that you may begin to live with Christ. Learn now to let go of all things so that you are free to go forward with Christ. Practice regular repentance so you will be confident in your relationship with God.

Only fools think they will live forever, although they can't guarantee themselves one more day. How many have been deceived by a false sense of security only to have it snatched away? How often do you hear about the sudden circumstances of someone's death? Someone was killed. Someone drowned. Someone broke their neck falling from some high place. Someone died while eating. Someone died playing. Someone died in a fire. Someone died in battle. Someone was killed by a disease. Someone was murdered during a robbery. Death awaits us all.

When you die, you die quickly and are gone forever. Who's going to remember you when you are dead? Who's going to pray for you then? Do what you can now while you are alive because you don't know when you are going to die. You have the time now to live life as God created it to be lived. Now is the time to make friends with deeply spiritual Christians, learning to imitate their actions; these will be the people who welcome you home to heaven.

Don't get too friendly and comfortable with this world. Your citizenship is in heaven. Keep your heart free and lifted up to God. Pray daily and cry out to God from your heart that when you die your relationship with Him will carry you happily from this world into the Lord's presence.

24 Living Beyond Self means understanding judgment for sin

In everything you do, keep in mind that someday you will stand before a judge who sees all things. Gifts and excuses cannot sway Him. He will judge you rightly and fairly. Why do you sometimes cower in fear when a person is angry with you while at the same time you don't know the answer you will give to God of what you've done wrong? Why are you not preparing your soul for that Day of Judgment, when you'll stand alone before God answering for yourself? Now is the time for confession and repentance. Now is the time for restoring your relationship with God.

Patient people seek to be pure before God. Though someone may hurt them, they are more concerned about the one who has caused them pain rather than focusing on being hurt. Patient people pray for their enemies and forgive from the heart when offended. They don't delay in asking forgiveness when they've done something wrong and they are more easily moved to compassion rather than anger. They discipline themselves to be less worldly and work fervently to submit themselves daily to the leadership of the Holy Spirit. It's better to cut out sinning now rather than to be cut off from God for eternity. Sadly, too many people love this world and themselves too much.

Stop sinning now and be sorry for your sins so that on the Day of Judgment you will be at peace. On that day, the righteous will stand with great boldness, the poor and humble will have great confidence, and the proud will be afraid and insecure. Then all will know that the truly wise person was the one who was despised because he or she was a fool for Jesus. On that day, all troubles, trials, and tribulations that believers have endured will end and they will possess the prize! You will see that every time you rejected this world and turned to Christ it was the right decision. Your old beaten up clothes will shine so gloriously that expensive designer clothes of today will be like dirty rags. Your modest lifestyle will be more worthy than any lavish lifestyle on earth. Your constant patience on earth will be more useful than any earthly power. Simple obedience will be exalted over all worldly wisdom. A good and clear conscience will be handier than all philosophical learning.

The simple life will weigh more than the entire world's treasure. You will be glad that you prayed more devoutly instead of wasting your time on trivial things. You will be glad that you kept silent more than talking too much. Your godly works will outweigh many good deeds. Accustom yourself to suffer a little now so that you will then be delivered from something far worse. Live this life in such a way that you will be prepared for the next. If you can't endure any hardship now, can you imagine being cut off from God for eternity?

You can't have your cake and eat it too; you can't indulge in this world and reign with Christ in the next. Suppose that you lived the high life, full of power and popularity. What good would this do you if you died right now and weren't prepared to meet God? That's why everything you can cling to in this life is ultimately pointless, except to love God and serve Him only. The person who loves God with his or her whole heart is not afraid of death, punishment, judgment, or hell. There is no fear in love for God's perfect love drives away all fear. You shouldn't be surprised that the person who delights in sin fears these things. There is small good in this, for if God's love hasn't convinced you yet, perhaps the fear of hell will hold you back from sinning. However, if you come to the place where you no longer stand in holy respect before God, you will quickly fall into the devil's hands and things will start going wrong in your life.

25 Living Beyond Self means surrendering your whole self to God

Give your undivided attention to serving God and remember why you chose to leave the world behind in favor of Christian community. Wasn't it because you loved God and wanted to grow spiritually? Make every effort to be completely God's, and it won't take long before you will start experiencing the benefits of this goal, and you also won't be sad or afraid at the hour of your death. Work a little now and you will end up with eternal rest and joy.

Continue to be faithful and fervent in your work, confident that God will be faithful and generous in rewarding you. Believe you will be victorious over sinfulness, but stay on guard because pride will make you lazy.

One day a man, who waffled between hope and fear in his relationship with God, felt depressed. He knelt in humble prayer before the altar of a church. While meditating on these things, he said, "If I only knew whether I will make it to heaven!" Instantly he heard the divine answer within saying, "If you knew this, what would you do? Do now what you would do then and you will be confident." Immediately consoled and comforted, he obeyed and the anxiety disappeared. He wasn't curious about what the future held for him anymore. He focused on finding the will of God in the present moment. As David said, *"Trust in the LORD and do good. Then you will live safely in the land and prosper"* (Psalm 37:3, NLT).

One thing that draws many back from growing in their faith and from continuing to pursue serious spiritual growth is the dread of difficulty and the toil of spiritual warfare. Obviously, those who bravely undertake the most difficult and unpleasant tasks far outpace others in the pursuit of godliness. A person makes the most progress and receives the most grace precisely in those areas where he or she gains the greatest victories over self—dying to self-will. It's true that the difficulties are different for each person, but the diligent and sincere person will make greater progress, even if he or she has more issues and obstacles than the person who is even-tempered but less concerned about godliness.

The two things that most enable spiritual growth are: (1) withdrawing yourself forcibly from those vices to which your human nature is most seriously inclined, and (2) working fervently for the good which we want most. Also, avoid finding faults in others and overcome letting them bother you. Make the best of every opportunity. If you see or hear of a good example, imitate it in your life. Be careful that you're not guilty of those things that you consider wrong. If you are guilty of them, correct your course as soon as possible. As you view others, so they view you. It is a true blessing to know a devout Christian who is passionate, mature, and disciplined! How sad and painful it is to see people wandering around confused, not fulfilling the purpose to which they are called! It hurts them to focus on things not meant for them!

Never forget your purpose and keep in mind the picture of the crucified Christ. Even though you may have walked for many years on God's path, you may be ashamed if, with the image of the crucified Christ as your example, you do not try to become more like Him daily. The serious person who concerns himself or herself intently with the life and passion of Jesus Christ will find everything that he or she needs and more. There is no need to seek for anything better than Jesus. If the crucified Christ would come into people's hearts, how quickly and abundantly they would learn!

A fervent Christian takes and bears all things well that is commanded by God. A negligent and lukewarm Christian has trial upon trial, suffers in many ways because this person has no inner peace, and is forbidden to seek it from the world. The disciple who does continue to grow

Book 2
Developing a Heart for God

1 Living Beyond Self means tending to your spiritual heart

Jesus said, "*The kingdom of God is within you*" (Luke 17:21). If you turn to the Lord with your whole heart and let go of this sinful world, your soul will find rest. Learn to let go of outward things that bring temporary satisfaction and instead put your energy into internal things that bring lasting peace. That's when you'll find the kingdom of God within you. "*For the kingdom of God is . . . peace and joy in the Holy Spirit*" (Romans 14:17) and you won't find it in unholy things.

Imagine you are a mansion for Jesus to live in with the fullness of His peace. All His glory and beauty begins with your inner life and you'll find that He takes pleasure in meeting you there. He enjoys speaking gentle words of peace and true friendship directly to your heart. Faithful Christian, open your heart to Jesus who loves you like His bride, and He'll fulfill His promise to come and dwell with you! For He promised: "*Anyone who loves me will obey my teaching . . . and we will come to them and make our home with them*" (John 14:23, TNIV). Therefore, open your life to Jesus only and let nothing else take His place. With Christ you are rich. He will help you faithfully in everything, so much so that you will no longer need to depend on people. People change often and fail you quickly. Christ remains forever and is your rock until the end.

You can't put this kind of trust into even the best of all human beings, even though in many ways people can help you. You also shouldn't be to upset when people, even those closest to you, disagree with you. You shouldn't place too much stock in those that are on your side today either, for tomorrow they may be against you. People change as often as the wind. Put your trust in God and honor Him only. Make God your first love and you'll see Him stand up for you, and do what's best for you in every situation.

You are not a permanent resident of this world. Wherever you are on this earth, you are a stranger and a pilgrim. You will not find rest in this world unless you are inwardly united with Christ. Why do you keep looking for something in this world to fulfill you, since this world can't offer you peace? Your citizenship is in heaven. All things on earth are temporary. All things pass away, and so will you. Beware that you don't cling to them, or they might keep you from eternal life with God. Focus your mind on God and prayerfully put your trust in a merciful Christ.

If you are having a difficult time thinking about God's good and beautiful things, you can always focus on the sacrifice of Christ and choose to live life as a servant. Take on the suffering servant nature of Jesus and then you'll be at peace in the midst of great trials. Then when people reject or ignore you, you won't be too bothered; words meant to hurt you will not penetrate your heart.

When Jesus was in the world, many people hated Him. Jesus, in the hour of His greatest need, was abandoned and denied by His closest friends. Christ was willing to suffer this hate and rejection, so why should you, His disciple, complain when similar things happen to you? Christ had enemies, so why do you hope all people will be your friends and want the best for you? How will you develop deep patience if you never experience adversity? If you aren't willing to face opposition or adversity, how can you be the friend of Christ? Suffer with Christ and for Christ if you desire to reign with Christ.

Enter totally into a deep inner conversation with Jesus and discover His passionate love. Don't think about things being easy or hard for you. Instead, be joyful when slanderers attack you, for a true love of Jesus makes a person desire to have his or her worldly concerns crucified with Christ. A true lover of Jesus, an inward Christian free from uncontrolled desires, can freely offer himself or herself to God, raise his or her spirit up above the bad circumstances of life, and remain in joyful peace.

The one who learns to see things as they really are and not just what others tell him or her is wise and taught by God. The person who is always living from the overflow of his or her heart, showing little concern for the outward things, has truly discovered wisdom and does not need a specific place or time for his or her devotional life. A spiritual person can gather himself or herself quickly and be in tune with God because he or she is never totally engaged in outward situations. This person does not disconnect from God when doing manual labor or business, which may be necessary for the time. Whatever the circumstances, this person is able to adjust positively.

The person who develops his or her spiritual heart

and maturity does not focus on the confusion and perversity of this world. A person's disconnectedness from God is directly related to how much he or she gets entangled with worldly concerns. If you are at peace and your heart is pure, all things would work together for your good and your growth. But if you often seem displeased and troubled, this is because your old sinful self isn't totally dead to this world. Nothing will defile you and confuse your heart like impure love. When you discover that you need nothing from anyone or anything in this world, you will be able to reflect on the things of heaven and experience internal joy.

2 Living Beyond Self means bringing everything to God in humility

Do not worry about trying to figure out who is for you or against you. Be concerned about your integrity, and make sure you see that God is with you in everything you do. A clear conscience is a sure way to know that God is on your side. With God as your defender, people's sinfulness will be unable to hurt you. Be patient and trusting and God will prove faithful in helping you. He alone knows the best time and method to deliver you, so trust yourself to His care. It is God's nature to help and deliver us from all confusion. Besides, it is often good for our own humility that others know and point out our faults.

When people humbly acknowledge their faults, it has a calming effect on others, and quickly satisfies those who are upset. God protects the humble and delivers them. He loves and comforts them. He prefers the humble person, and raises such a person up after a humiliation. God reveals His secrets to the humble and gently invites and draws the humble to himself. Even when a humble person is confused, he or she is at peace because his or her trust is in God and not this world. Do not think that you have made any spiritual progress unless you think of yourself as the servant of others.

3 Living Beyond Self means you must be a person of peace

If you want to be at peace with others you must first be at peace. A peaceful person often does more good than a well-educated person does. On the contrary, a person dominated by passion often draws even the good people into evil and easily believes worst-case scenarios. A peaceful person turns all things to good and believes the best about others. The person who is discontent and troubled is suspicious of others, stirred up on the inside, and causes disturbances in others. This kind of person often says things he or she shouldn't say out loud and then leaves out details that would make himself or herself look bad. Such a person obsesses over what other people ought to do and neglects what he or she should be doing. That's why first, and foremost, you need to tend to your own life. Then you may be able to help your neighbor in doing right.

You're really good at making excuses for yourself and

making yourself look good. Why do you get angry when others do the same thing? It's better if you point the finger at yourself instead of others. Since people have to put up with your antics, you should be patient with theirs. Think about how far away you are from unconditional love and humility—the kind of character that doesn't easily anger and isn't easily frustrated, unless it's pointed toward one's self. Don't think you're so great because you hang out with good and gentle people; everybody likes that. Everyone enjoys harmony and loves best the people that agree with them. To be able to live peacefully with hard and perverse persons—people whose lives are disorderly and who disagree with us—is a great grace and a most admirable and honorable characteristic.

Some people are at peace with themselves and with others and spend time reflecting on how to spread that peace to others. Some are inwardly restless and spread anxiety and trouble. However, they are always more troublesome to themselves. However, true peace in this life does not mean you will face no challenges. True peace means you know how to bear all things with patience and humility. The person who does this best will be the person who lives most peacefully in this world. Such a person conquerors self, is an overcomer of the world, a friend of Christ, and a child of heaven.

4 Living Beyond Self means having a single focus

A person rises above this world through developing simplicity and purity. Simplicity is the compass for your choices; purity is the compass for your desires. Simplicity means trust and reliance on God; purity means fulfillment and joy in God. No good act that you attempt will be fruitless if you are free from worldly desires. If your focus is nothing else but the will of God and the good of your neighbor, you will experience the joy of true freedom. If your heart is sincere and upright, then all people and all creation become a looking glass of life and a book of holy doctrine. There is nothing in creation that is too small or insignificant that it does not represent the goodness of God.

If your heart is good and pure, then you'll see and understand everything without confusion. A pure heart penetrates heaven and hell. People view the outside world by the character of their heart. If there is any joy in the world, a person with a pure heart will notice and grab hold of it. If there is any trouble and pain in the world, a person with a sin-dominated conscience will find it. As iron put into the fire loses its rust and becomes clearly red hot, so a person who wholly turns himself or herself over to God will put off all laziness and apathy and become a new person. You know a person is growing lukewarm when he or she begins to back away from sacrifice and hard work, looking for comfort in people or things. However, when people begin to overcome themselves consistently and walk with strength in the way of God, then the things that used to matter so much suddenly won't seem like such a big deal.

5 Living Beyond Self means trusting in God, not yourself

Some people can't trust their judgment too much because they lack understanding and aren't living fully in God's grace. They even tend to lose the understanding they have because of neglect. They simply don't realize how blind they truly are. They do evil and make it worse by making excuses for why they do it. They occasionally get excited emotionally and think this means they're on fire for God. They get too irritated with the small faults of others and pass over bigger faults within themselves. They're quick to dwell on the discomfort and suffering that others cause them and fail to think about how they contribute to the problems. People who consider carefully their own lives won't judge other people too harshly.

Christians who've developed hearts for God focus first on their own spiritual lives above all other things and easily keep quiet about others. You will never be deeply Christian until you can pass over other's faults silently, preferring to mull over your own instead. If you spend your time being wholly devoted to God and living Christ's life, you won't be anxious about what is happening around you. You always have to live with yourself. If you spend time running around correcting everyone else but yourself, what good is that? If you desire peace of mind and purity of purpose, you must quit judging others and focus on your own growth.

When you're free from earthly concerns, you'll make great spiritual progress. Yet, you'll find yourself falling fast if you become too concerned with earthly things. Nothing is important, nothing is exalted, nothing is pleasing, nothing is acceptable except God alone and anything God brings into your life. Do not care too much for life's comforts or peoples' approval. A soul that loves God can let go of all things that are inferior to God. God alone is everlasting and of infinite greatness, filling all creatures. God alone is the soul's home and the true joy of the heart.

6 Living Beyond Self means experiencing the joy of a good conscience

A good life comes from a good conscience. If you have a good conscience, you will have joy. A good conscience helps you handle many challenges with a good attitude. An evil conscience is always fearful and unquiet. You can rest peacefully when you don't feel guilty. Never rejoice unless you have a reason to celebrate. Sinners never experience true joy or feel peace because "*There is no peace . . . for the wicked*" (Isaiah 48:22). If they try to tell you that they are at peace, that nothing bad can happen to them and that no one can hurt them, do not believe this for one second! They will experience the wrath of God in an instant, their deeds will prove empty, and their thoughts will pass away.

Glorifying God in suffering isn't hard for the person who loves. Living this way means living life from the perspective of the cross of Jesus. Glory that people give you is short lived and brings sorrow. The glory of the good is in their consciences and not in the praises of people. The gladness of the just is of God and in God; their joy is of the truth. Whoever wants real and lasting glory doesn't care about the temporary. Whoever seeks temporary glory, or whoever does not turn away from it in his or her heart, shows that he or she doesn't truly think highly of the glory of heaven. Peaceful people don't care much about the praises or insults of people.

The person with a pure conscience will be content in all things. Even though this is a good thing, remember you're never as holy as you think you are. At the same time, your faults never make you as unworthy as you sometimes feel because of them. You are what you are and no words of people can make you greater in God's sight. If you consider who you really are and what God thinks of you, you will no longer care what people think about you! People look at your appearance, but God looks at your heart. People judge you by your accomplishments, but God considers your motives.

Being in a constant state of peace and not thinking too highly of yourself is a sign of a humility. Refusing to find comfort from people is a sign of great purity and inward confidence. The person who doesn't try to get people to praise them in front of others shows that they have committed themselves completely to God. As Paul says, *"For it is not those who commend themselves that are ap-*

proved, but those whom the Lord commends" (2 Corinthians 10:18, TNIV). Developing a deep relationship with God and resisting all other competitors for your soul is the sign of a person who is living Christ's life.

7 Living Beyond Self means loving Jesus more than anyone or anything

You're blessed when you love Jesus more than anyone or anything, especially yourself. It's a great thing to put your love for Jesus before your own need for love. For the love we receive from any created thing is deceitful and/or inconsistent, while the love of Jesus is faithful and persevering. The one who latches on to earthly things is entangled in his or her human imperfections. The one who embraces Jesus stands firm forever. Love Jesus and make Him your best friend. When all others abandon you, He will not forsake you, nor allow you to perish in the end. At some point you will be separated from all things in this world through death, as no one lives in this world forever.

Keep close to Jesus in both life and death, and commit yourself to His trust. When all else fails, He alone can help you. This is Jesus' nature. He will allow no rivals. He alone wants first place in your life and to sit on the throne of your heart as king. If you could empty yourself perfectly from all earthly love, Jesus would willingly make His home in you. Taking comfort in people and not Jesus is a waste of your time and energy. Trust not, nor lean upon, a reed full of wind. All flesh is grass, and the glory of this life will wither away as the flower of the field. You'll be quickly deceived if you only look at people as they appear to be. If you seek comfort and profit from others, you will often feel loss. If you seek Jesus in all things, you will surely find Jesus there. However, if you seek yourself, you will find yourself, and this leads to destruction. You do more hurt to yourself by not seeking Jesus than the whole world and all your adversaries can do to you.

8 Living Beyond Self means keeping company with Jesus

In Jesus' presence all is well and nothing seems too difficult. When Jesus is absent, everything seems hard. When people don't hear Jesus speaking inwardly to them, all other comfort is worthless. However, if Jesus merely speaks one word to them, they feel great peace. Didn't Mary rise immediately from the place where she wept, when Martha said to her, "*The Teacher is here...and is asking for you*" (John 11:28)? What joy there is when Jesus turns sadness into spiritual peace!

People become dry and hard without Jesus! How foolish it is to desire anything outside of Jesus! Isn't it worse to lose Jesus than if you would lose the whole world? What good can the world be to you without Jesus? To be without Jesus is hell on earth; to be with Jesus is heaven on earth. If Jesus is with you, no enemy can hurt you. The person who finds Jesus finds a good treasure—the true good above all good. Whoever loses Jesus loses much; indeed, they lose more than the whole world! Real poverty is life without Jesus; real wealth is life with Jesus.

It is a matter of practice to know how to hold a conversation with Jesus, and to know how to stay in conversation with Jesus is priceless. Be humble and peaceable and Jesus will be with you. Be devout and quiet in your heart and Jesus will stay with you. You may soon drive Jesus away and lose contact with His voice if you turn your attention to outside things. And if you should drive His voice away from you and lose touch with Him, whom will you turn to then? Whom will you seek for your friend? Without true friends, you cannot live well. If Jesus is not above all your truest friend, you will be sad and empty. It is not wise to trust or rejoice in any other. It's better to have the whole world against you than to ignore Jesus.

Out of all the people that are especially dear to you, let us make sure that Jesus is the one you love the most. Love all people as Jesus loves them and love Jesus for himself. Jesus Christ alone is worthy of your love. He alone is good and faithful above all friends. For Him and in Him, let your friends and your enemies be dear to your heart. Pray that everyone would know and love Jesus. Never desire places of popularity and prestige above other people, only God deserves this kind of recognition. You shouldn't desire that the heart of any person be fixed on you, nor should you fix your heart on the love of another. Let Jesus be in you and see Him in every good person.

Be pure, free within, and don't allow your heart to be entangled with any person. You must be totally open before God, ever presenting your heart purely toward Him if you really want to be free and to see and experience how sweet the Lord is. In fact, unless you are drawn by His grace-that-goes-before you, you will never reach the happiness of forsaking and leaving all for the sake of being united to Him alone. When God's grace comes like this to a person, he or she is capable of anything. When it seems far away, the person is weak, and left in a desperate and lonely state. If this should happen to you, do not sink into dejection or despair, but stand steadily in God's will. Whatever comes upon you, endure it for the glory of Jesus Christ. Remember, after winter comes summer, after night comes day, and after a storm comes a great calm.

9 Living Beyond Self means finding comfort in God alone

It's not too hard to let go of human comfort when you've experienced divine comfort. However, it is a good thing if you can live without either human or divine comfort. You must, for the glory of God, endure patiently the exile of the heart—not seeking self or what you feel you deserve. It is a great thing to be found cheerful and devout when the God of grace comes. All people hope they are this strong. Whomever the grace of God sustains travels peacefully in this life. It is no marvel that a person doesn't feel burdened, for he or she is carried by God and led by the His guidance.

It's human to want something for one's comfort and it

is not easy to strip oneself of self interest. The holy martyr Lawrence, along with his priest, overcame the world because he did not delight in what the world delighted in. For the love of Jesus Christ the Roman deacon Lawrence patiently endured when his Christian friend Sixtus, whom he dearly loved, was taken away from him. He sought the love of the Creator rather than comfort of humankind. You too must learn to part with an intimate and important friendship love for the love of God. Do not take it too hard when a friend deserts you. Remember that in the end everyone faces his or her death alone before God.

    A person must learn to fight long and bravely against "self" before he or she can learn to master "self" and direct all affections toward God. When you trust in yourself, you will rely on human comfort. A true lover of Christ, who sincerely pursues virtue, does not fall back on any comfort and doesn't seek any pleasure he or she could hold on to, but prefers trials and hard work for the sake of Jesus Christ.

    When God gives you spiritual comfort, receive it gratefully, but remember that it is His gift and not something you earned. Do not be proud of yourself, do not be overjoyed, and do not presume that you earned it; but allow the gift to make you more reliant on God. Be more careful in your actions, for this hour will pass and temptation will come again. When the comforting feeling is taken away, do not get depressed. Wait humbly and patiently for another heavenly visit, since God can give you another even greater comfort. This is no new teaching or strange way of life to the spiritually experienced and mature, for such change of circumstance was common for the great saints and prophets of old.

Enjoying a grace-filled time the psalmist said "*in my prosperity, 'I will never be moved'*" (Psalm 30:6, NASB). However, when grace appeared removed he said, "*You hid your face, [and] I was dismayed*" (Psalm 30:7, NASB). Yet, he didn't despair, but rather prayed more earnestly, "*To You, O LORD, I called, And to the Lord I made supplication*" (Psalm 30:8, NASB). Through long-suffering, he received the fruit of his prayer and testified: "*Hear, O LORD, and be gracious to me; O LORD, be my helper*" (Psalm 30:10 NASB). The prophet responded to the Lord's answer to his prayer: "*You have turned my mourning into dancing...*" [and have surrounded] *me with gladness*" (Psalm 30:11, NASB).

If the great saints had to go through this, you who are weak and poor ought not to despair that sometimes you are on fire for God and at other times less passionate. For the Spirit comes and goes according to His will and you cannot control this. About the Spirit, Job the blessed said: "*You examine him early in the morning and test him every moment*" (Job 7:18).

Where can you find hope? Who can you trust? Seek the great mercy of God and the hope of heavenly grace. For though you are surrounded by good people, devout Christians, faithful friends, holy books, beautiful writings, sweet songs and hymns, all these truly help and please you little when the grace of God leaves you to your poverty of spirit. At such times, the best remedy is patience and surrendering yourself to the care of God.

I never found any person that was so devout that

when he or she had a moment of despair did not also feel some decrease in spiritual zeal. There was never a saint that was so caught up in God's spirit and enlightened that he or she was not able to be tempted. Indeed, one is not worthy of the gift of contemplation of God who has not experienced some tribulation for the sake of God. Temptation is often the sign that precedes the comfort of grace to follow. Heavenly consolation is promised to all those proved by the fire of temptation. Christ said that for those who overcome, He "*will give the right to eat from the tree of life*" (Revelation 2:7). Divine comfort is given in order to make a person braver in enduring adversity and temptation in order that he or she may not become prideful in the good that he or she accomplishes. The devil doesn't sleep and the flesh is not yet dead. Therefore, you must never cease your preparation for battle, because on the right and on the left are enemies who never rest.

10 Living Beyond Self means cultivating gratitude for God's grace

Why do you seek rest when you were born to work? Pursue patience rather than comfort and learn to bear the Cross rather than pursue happiness. What worldly person is there that would not willingly receive spiritual joy and comfort if he or she could always feel it? Spiritual comforts exceed all the delights of the world and pleasures of the flesh. All worldly delights are at best temporary, or at worst unclean. However, spiritual delights are pleasant and honest, sprung from virtue, and infused by God into pure minds. But no person can always enjoy these divine comforts whenever he or she so desires, for times of temptation are always possible. People's false sense of freedom and over-confidence in themselves is contrary to heavenly grace. God is good in giving people graceful comfort, but they do evil in not giving everything back to God with thanksgiving. Therefore, the gifts of grace cannot flow in others, because they are unthankful to the Giver. Grace is always present to the thankful. Whatever the proud have now will be taken from them and given to the humble.

I do not desire any comfort that would diminish the Spirit's conviction, nor do I aspire to a spiritual life that would make me prideful. For all that is high in the world is not holy, not everything that is sweet is good, every desire is not pure, and everything people hold dear is not pleasing to God. Willingly I accept the grace that makes me more humble, more in awe of God, and more ready to renounce myself. Whoever is taught by the gift of grace and disciplined by the withdrawing of grace learns not to attribute any good to themselves but rather acknowledges themselves as poor and naked.

Give to God that which is God's and give to yourself that which belongs to you. That is, give thanks to God for His grace and acknowledge any sin you might have not confessed. Always choose the lowest place and God will give the highest to you, for the higher cannot stand without the lower. The chief saints before God are the least in their own estimations of themselves. Those that are full of truth and heavenly glory do not desire personal glory. Those that are settled and grounded in God can in no way be proud. A wise person gives credit to God in everything and for whatever good he or she receives. This person does not seek glory from people, but wishes for that glory which comes from God alone. This person desires above all things that God may be praised; this is the continuous pursuit of his or her life. People like this are the ones who truly know God.

Be thankful, then, for the smallest gift so you will be ready to receive a greater one. Let the least be as important to you as the greatest. View even the most worthless gift as one of special value. If you consider the worth of the giver, no gift will seem too small or worthless. Nothing that is given by God can be small or worthless. Even if you receive punishment and illness, it ought to become an opportunity for thankfulness because God works all things together for the good of those who love Him—even the things He permits to happen to us. Whoever desires to accept the grace of God should be thankful for grace given and patient when it appears withdrawn. Let him or her pray that grace becomes full and abundant in his or her life.

11 Living Beyond Self means being counted among the few that truly love the Cross

Jesus has many people who love Him because they want to go to heaven, but few who willingly bear His cross. He has many who desire comfort from Him, but few who willingly accept trials. He has many companions who wish to join Him at the table, but few who accept His Father's discipline. All desire to rejoice with Him, but few are willing to endure anything for Him or with Him. Many follow Jesus only to the breaking of the bread, but few follow Him to the drinking of the cup of His suffering. Many revere His miracles yet few follow Him through to the disgrace of the Cross. Many love Jesus so long as no adversities come to them. Many praise and bless Him as long as they receive something from Him. But if the blessings disappear from their lives even for a little while, they fall either into complaining or into depression. But those who love Jesus for the sake of Jesus, and not for something special they get from Him, bless Him in all trials and anguish of heart as if they were in perfect peace. Even if Jesus promised them no comfort, they would still praise Him and seek always to give thanks.

O how perfect is the pure love of Jesus, which is mixed with no self-interest or self-love. After all, wouldn't you consider those who are always seeking something for their services "mercenaries"? Don't spiritual mercenaries show themselves to be lovers of self rather than lovers of Christ, always thinking of their own profit and advantage? Show me one person who is willing to serve God for nothing in return! Rarely is anyone found so spiritual as to be stripped of all things. How often do you ever find a person who is poor in spirit and thoroughly absent of any need for approval from others? A person such as this is not easily found. If a person were to give God everything he or she had, it would amount to nothing. If a person practiced great repentance, it would amount to little. If a person attained all the knowledge in the world, he or she would still be far away. Even if he or she had great virtue and very fervent devotions, there would still be much they needed, especially one essential thing. What is that? Leaving all, forsaking self, and giving one's whole life—holding nothing back out of self-love. Even when all that has been done, as far as it is possible to know this, a person should still consider that his or her work amounts to nothing.

Do not care too much about being considered important by others. Simply recognize yourself as an unprofitable servant, as Jesus himself said: "*When you have done everything you were told to do, you should say, 'We are unworthy servants'*" (Luke 17:10). Then you may be truly poor and naked in spirit, saying with the prophet, "*I am alone and in deep distress*" (Psalm 25:16, NLT). Yet in truth, this is precisely when there is no one richer than you, no one more powerful, and no one more free; for you are now able to leave yourself and all things and choose to be the servant of all.

12 Living Beyond Self means following the path of Jesus

Jesus' words "*Whoever wants to be my disciple must deny themselves and take up their cross and follow me*" (Matthew 16:24, TNIV) seem too difficult for most people. In truth, it would be much harder to hear Jesus say, "*De-

part from me, you who are cursed, into the eternal fire" (Matthew 25:41). If you hear the Word and follow the way of the Cross now, you never have to worry about judgment. The sign of the Cross will be clearly seen in heaven on the Day of Judgment. On that day all of God's servants who conformed themselves to the crucified Christ during their lives will draw near to Him with great confidence.

Why are you afraid to take up the Cross that leads to the kingdom of God? In the Cross is salvation, life, protection from our enemies, heavenly peace, strength of mind, joy of spirit, height of virtue, and the perfection of sanctity. There is no salvation of soul or hope of everlasting life but in the Cross. So take up your cross and follow Jesus and you will go into everlasting life. Jesus went before you and suffered and died on the Cross so that you would desire to bear your cross and die with Him. If you die with Him, you will also live with Him. If you are His companion unto death then you will also be His companion in glory.

There is nothing apart from the Cross, and your whole life depends on your dying on the Cross! There is no other way to life and peace, except through the way of the Cross. You may choose to act according to your own will and wisdom, but you will always discover that some suffering will come, whether you want it to or not. Willing or not, maybe through bodily pain or a troubled spirit, you will discover the Cross. Sometimes God will seem distant, sometimes those around you will trouble you, and more often than not, you'll be a burden to yourself!

There is no easy answer for such trials and tribulations. You must learn to bear them with patience as long as God allows them to be in your life. God wants you to learn that life and discipleship are not always comfortable. He also wants you to learn that the only way to live is through the surrender of everything to Him. Through your suffering you will become more humble. No person will ever suffer as much as Christ. The way of the Cross is always available for you to choose. You can't escape it even if you try to run away from it. Above and below, within and without, wherever you turn you will find the Cross. Always and everywhere be patient in suffering if you want inward peace and an everlasting crown. If you willingly carry the Cross, it will carry you and lead you to where there is no more suffering—though that won't be found here on earth. If you bear the Cross unwillingly, it will become a burden and increase your load, but you'll still have to bear it. If you cast away one cross, you will surely pick up another, and that cross may be even harder to bear.

Why do you imagine you can escape the suffering that is common to every human being? Name one of the saints who have not had their crosses and tribulations! Not even our Lord Jesus Christ ever had an hour without suffering and death on His mind. According to Jesus *"the Christ will suffer and rise from the dead"* (Luke 24:46) and` enter into His glory.

Why do you presume to find some other way than this royal way, the way of the Cross? Christ's whole life was a cross and martyrdom, so why do you seek only joy and rest for yourself? You are deceived if you seek any other thing. This life is full of tribulations, miseries, and suffering. Often the higher a person advances in the spiritual life, the heavier the crosses he or she has to bear. Temporary struggles lead to greater love of God. Though afflicted in many ways, a person is not without comfort knowing that bearing of the Cross will ultimately bring its reward. As a person accepts the Cross, the burden of tribulation is replaced by the confidence of divine comfort. The more the flesh is destroyed by affliction, the more the spirit is strengthened by inward grace. Sometimes such a person is so comforted with the desire of tribulation and adversity because he or she wants to conform to the cross of Christ. This person cannot wish to be without grief or troubles because such a person believes he or she will be a more perfect vessel for God's use the more he or she suffers for Him. This is not human ability or strength, but it is the grace of Christ, which can and does so much in frail flesh. So powerful is this grace that it enables the person to encounter and love what he or she would naturally flee and reject.

You are not naturally inclined as a human being to love and bear the Cross, to discipline your body and mind through fasting and prayer, to flee the praises of people, to willingly suffer, to despise selfishness, to be seen as flawed, to endure all adversities and damages, and to desire no prosperity in this world. If you look to yourself, you will be able to accomplish nothing of this kind. But if you trust in the Lord, you will receive the fortitude of heaven, and the world and the flesh will be subject to your command. You will not fear your enemy the devil if you are armed with faith and marked with the cross of Christ.

Imagine yourself as a good and faithful servant of Christ. Bear courageously the cross of your Lord who, out of love, was crucified for you. Prepare yourself to bear many adversities and troubles in this life as they will be with you wherever you are—you cannot hide from them. There is no way to escape tribulation and sorrow, but there is a means to make it through. Drink from the Lord's cup with great love if you desire to be His friend and to be united with Him. Leave all comforts to God and let Him do as He sees fit. You should be concerned with preparing for tribulations and learning to accept them as the greatest comforts. Present sufferings pale in comparison with the glory to come. When you come to this state of mind, even when tribulation seems sweet and you relish it for Christ's sake, you will know that all is well for you because you have found paradise on earth. As long as trouble and suffering grieves you, and you desire to flee it, you will live uneasily on this earth and fear will follow you everywhere.

If you fix your mind on accepting suffering willingly, even to the point of death, things will quickly be better in your soul and you will find peace. Just like Paul, you are not free from adversity in this life. Jesus said about Paul, "*I will show him how much he must suffer for my name*" (Acts 9:16). You now know that you will suffer. Therefore, choose to love Jesus and serve Him always. It is a great thing for you to be counted worthy to suffer for the name of Jesus! You would understand the greatness of glory, inspire joy among all the saints of God, and be an encouragement to your neighbors. All people speak of needing patience, but few are willing to suffer. You ought to approach the smallest suffering cheerfully for Christ's sake, since many suffer worse things for the world.

Know for certain that you ought to lead a "dying life." The more you die to yourself, the more you begin to live for God. No person is fit to comprehend heavenly things until he or she is able to submit to bearing adversities for Christ's sake. Nothing is more acceptable to God or more worthwhile for you in this world than to suffer cheerfully for Christ. If you could choose, you ought to be more inclined to choose suffering than comfort, because this would make you more like Christ and the saints. For your strength and spiritual growth is not formed in comfort, but rather through the challenge of enduring afflictions and tribulations. Indeed, if there were some better way that was more profitable for humanity's salvation than suffering, surely Christ would have showed it by word and example. For both the disciples that followed Jesus and all who still desire to follow Him, He plainly says to them, *"Whoever wants to be my disciple must deny themselves and take up their cross and follow me"* (Luke 9:23). When you have thoroughly read and searched all paths, let this be the final conclusion: you *"must go through many hardships to enter the kingdom of God"* (Acts 14:22).

www.ingramcontent.com/pod-product-compliance
Lightning Source LLC
Chambersburg PA
CBHW061338040426
42444CB00011B/2973